Nicolai Westsee

Analysis of the German and European Electric Power Market

GRIN Verlag

Bibliografische Information der Deutschen Nationalbibliothek:

Die Deutsche Bibliothek verzeichnet diese Publikation in der Deutschen National-
bibliografie; detaillierte bibliografische Daten sind im Internet über http://dnb.d-
nb.de/ abrufbar.

Imprint:

Copyright © 2013 GRIN Verlag GmbH
Druck und Bindung: Books on Demand GmbH, Norderstedt Germany
ISBN: 978-3-656-62098-3

This book at GRIN:

http://www.grin.com/en/e-book/270581/analysis-of-the-german-and-european-
electric-power-market

GRIN - Your knowledge has value

Der GRIN Verlag publiziert seit 1998 wissenschaftliche Arbeiten von Studenten, Hochschullehrern und anderen Akademikern als eBook und gedrucktes Buch. Die Verlagswebsite www.grin.com ist die ideale Plattform zur Veröffentlichung von Hausarbeiten, Abschlussarbeiten, wissenschaftlichen Aufsätzen, Dissertationen und Fachbüchern.

Visit us on the internet:

http://www.grin.com/

http://www.facebook.com/grincom

http://www.twitter.com/grin_com

Leibniz Universität Hannover

Wirtschaftswissenschaftliche Fakultät

Institut für Wirtschaftsinformatik

Seminararbeit im Rahmen des Seminars

„Herausforderungen der Transformation des deutschen Energiesystems"

Sommersemester 2013

Analysis of the German and European Electric Power Market

Datum: 10.06.2013

Table of Content

List of Figures

List of Tables

List of Abbreviations

ACER	Agency for the Cooperation of Energy Regulators
cf.	confer (compare)
DNO	Distribution Network Operators
e.g.	exempli gratia (for example)
ed.	editor
et al.	et alii (and others)
EEX	European Energy Exchange
EFET	European Federation of Energy Traders
ENTSO	European Network of Transmission System Operators
EnWG	Energiewirtschaftsgesetz
EU	European Union
f.	and the following one
et seqq.	and the following
IEM	Internal Electricity Market
kWh	kilowatt-hour
MW	Megawatt
OTC	Over The Counter
R&D	Research and Development
RES	Renewable electricity
TSO	Transmission System Operators

1   Introduction

In the middle of the 19th century electricity began to dominate the life of all the generations
since then. It improved the quality of life and made it more comfortable and easy in many
areas. Nowadays life is unimaginable without electric power. Almost no means of transpor-
tation, no means of communication, and no computer system would work. Humanity became more and more dependent upon energy. The consumption increased over the years
and different markets arose to make this commodity tradable. The historical development,
the differences in the markets and the future of these markets are the focus of this seminar
paper.

Firstly some points for the general understanding of the connection of electricity, power
and energy: *Electricity* is the generic term of phenomena in conjunction with the flow of
electric charge. *Power* is the rate of flow of energy, which is measured in watts (W), kilo-
watts (kW), megawatts (MW), etc. *Energy* is an accumulation of power over a certain period of time, usually measured in kWh. One kilowatt flowing for one hour delivers one kWh,
which is the most common marking of energy load for final costumers (cf. Stoft, 2002, p.
30 f.).

In order to make the naturally available primary energies, such as wind- or sun power, fos-
sil-fuel or uranium usable for humankind, they need to be converted into secondary energy.
The secondary energy is transported to the customers by a comprehensive grid. The complex electricity-system includes the transformation of primary to secondary energy, as well
as the transmission grid and the distribution network for the end customers. Within this
complex system different instances are involved, to trade the energy. The private end customer usually pays per kWh. The price formation on the electric power market is influenced by factors like current load, availability of power plants, temperature, wind speed,
sunshine duration and the store capacity. The resulting price is highly dependent upon daily, weekly, monthly and annually cycles. In addition to that, the low substitutability and the
challenge to store large amounts of energy result in a high volatility of energy prices
(Borchert et al. 2006, p. 9).

The main goal of this term paper is to give an overview about differences within the European market and their advantages and disadvantages. Additionally the historical develop-

ment of energy markets and the future perspective, influenced by the development of the renewables shall be pointed out.

The next part, after this introduction, is about the historical development of the electric power market in Europe with a focus on the German market liberalization. In section three, the two different market models *Open-Market model* and *Pool-Market model* are discussed. After an explanation and a comparison of the two models, the trend towards renewables is taken into account. The focus lays on the development, the integration into the different existing electricity-markets in Germany and Spain and on their impacts on these markets.

Based on a study of Makkonen et al. from 2012, published in the journal *Energy Policy* an extensive outlook in future requirements, changes and possibilities of the development of a single European Electricity Market, this term paper will be concluded.

2   Development of the European Electric Power Market with Focus on Germany

The structuring of the German electric power market began with the first *Energiewirtschaftsgesetz* (EnWG, "economics of energy law") in 1935. Its primary goal was to ensure the feed-in with energy and the formation of a monopolistic market. It was expected to achieve a high level of planning security and the price was to be controlled by government (cf. Schemm et al. 2005, p. 80 f. and Borchert et al. 2006, p. 4 f.).

At that point the generation, the transmission, the distribution and the retail supply were provided by individual electric utilities and thus every one of these utilities had the exclusive market power in a specific geographical area (cf. Joskow, 2008, p. 10 f.). The reason for the elimination of competition in specific areas was the idea that energy supply will be more efficient and cheaper for the costumers. If there is only one regional provider, they alone will make investments in the grid-infrastructure. So the high costs for the grid expansion are carried by a monopolistic provider and parallel investments are avoided (cf. Schemm et al. 2005, p. 80 f. and von Koppenfels, 2010, p. 78 f.)

Some decades later, in 1990, the way of thinking changed towards a more liberalized energy market. The idea was to liberalize the market based on the model of the liberalization of the telecommunication market (cf. Borchert et al. 2006, p. 7 f. and von Koppenfels, 2010,

p. 79). The European Union decided to make the first step of the liberalization with the separation between the monopolistic structure of the grid on one side and other areas like generation, providing and distribution on the other side. The main goal was to guarantee free market access for all suppliers in order to stimulate competition (cf. von Koppenfels, 2010, p. 78 f.).

The first European liberalization package of measures was drafted in 1996 and 1998. Its main objective was to grant non-discriminating market access for generators to the power grid. This package was implemented on a very limited basis by the EU-member states and so the success was unsatisfying (cf. von Koppenfels, 2010, p. 79).

In 1998 the German government renewed the EnWG on basis of the prementioned first EU-liberalization draft, so that the legal background for a complete market-opening was achieved in Germany. This led to a crowding out of long-term delivery contracts. These contracts were very typical before the liberalization because only a few supplied the market, and so contracts of long duration were negotiated. After the first liberalization-package the long-term contracts got substituted more and more by short-term contracts, because the amount of competitors entering the market increased and a wide range of offers became available. On short-term markets the price formation is dominated by the interplay of supply and demand, which made the prices more dynamic (cf. Borchert et al. 2006, p. 7 f.).

A consequence of the liberalization was the necessity of the establishment of new market mechanisms. In 2002 the two German energy-stock-exchanges merged in the EEX with its headquarter in Leipzig, Germany. In the course of time the derivative trading grew in addition to the physical trading of energy (cf. Zenke and Schäfer, 2012, p. 1). So the EEX established a futures-market for the trading of financial products, which will be described more precisely in section 3.1. Because of the limited success of the first Liberalization package the EU increased their effort and in 2003 a second package of measures was adopted. The regulated grid access became mandatory, independent regulatory authorities became forbidden and vertically integrated suppliers had to divest some divisions in independent subsidiary companies (cf. von Koppenfels, 2012, p. 79 f.).

In 2005 the German government introduced the law-change into national legislation. The *Bundesnetzagentur* ("federal grid agency") became the sole responsibility to regulate the grid access tariffs as a central instance (cf. von Koppenfels, 2012, p. 80). Just as the first package, also the second one didn't fulfill the expectations completely. As a consequence the European commission for competition began with an extensive analysis of the existing competition barriers. Central findings of the analysis were the lack of transparency caused by missing and delayed information exchange, as well as the low stimulus to invest in the existing grids and finally the still existing market concentration of incumbent operators in their central markets (cf. von Koppenfels, 2012, p. 80 f.).

In 2007 the EU commission drafted the third package of measures to bring the market liberalization to success. This package included as the central point the unbundling between the transmission-grids and the business sectors generation, providing and distribution. According to the new regulations, the companies participating in these business sectors should no longer be allowed to hold shares on transmission companies. The strict separation was meant to solve the conflict of interests. As a result of this change a non-discriminating grid access was meant to be granted. The draft was debated heavily by the EU member states and finally a compromise was found, which was not as strict as what was being demanded by the EU (cf. von Koppenfels, 2012, p. 84 et seqq.). The positive outcome of the following wave of discussions was a general change in the minds of big energy companies. As a consequence, some of them declared the selling off of their grid infrastructure (cf. von Koppenfels, 2012, p. 89).

3   Differences in Electricity Market Models in Europe

Right after the Second World War many countries declared the nationalization of their oil and electricity companies to remain independent of others and to be able to fulfill the extreme dependence on energy to keep the machinery of war running for possible future wars (cf. Chick, 2007, p. 87).

After the Cold War, when the prospect of the necessity of an armament decreased, energy markets became more and more liberalized. In the European Union this process was initiated by the European Parliament and the European Council (cf. section 2). The directives didn't design a concrete market, but they fixed the frame conditions to develop a single *Internal Electricity Market* (IEM) (cf. Meeus et al. 2005, p. 26).

Trading with energy is linked to some special characteristics. Firstly electricity is heavily storable. This induces the difficulty to provide enough energy to cover the current demand. If the demand situation exceeds the current supply, not every request can be satisfied. Vice versa a higher supply can cause power system instability. Hence the challenge to keep the grid in a stable condition arises. Secondly, final consumers are almost price inelastic because a higher demand must be served at the same moment, a postproduction is impossible. Electricity is a homogenously commodity and the consumer obtains it not from a single supplier, the energy comes from an extensive grid, where nobody can ascertain who distributes to whom. These characteristics make it easy to trade energy. Only the input and the output inward and outward the grid needs to be acquired (cf. Ströbele et al. 2010, p. 229 f.).

The European Electric power market developed into two different directions. The outcome is firstly the open-market model and secondly the pool-market model. Table 1 below shows some different European countries or areas, their trading model and the names of their energy stock exchanges.

Table 1: European Energy Stock Exchanges and different Market Models

Country	Market model	Energy stock exchange
Germany	open	EEX (European Energy Exchange)
Netherlands	open	APX (Power Spot Exchange)
Italy	open	GME (Gestore Mercati Energetici)
France	open	Powernext
Scandinavia	Pool	NordPool
Spain	Pool	Omel (Operador del Mercado Ibérico de Energía)

Source: cf. Ströbele et al. 2010, p. 229.

3.1   The Open-Market Model

The open-market-model allows the trading of one good, in this case electricity, on different and strictly separated markets. The main reason for opening electricity markets is to support competition. The supply chain of power is composed of many elements, like electricity generation, transmission, energy distribution and at least electric energy supply. An increase in competition, may lead to an increase in the customers benefits as well. But competition is not desired in all of these elements; to avoid bottlenecks and blackouts, the functions related to the network infrastructure and transmission services will remain under monopoly (cf. Arus, 2013).

The open-market market is more than just an organized market in the classical sense, where demand and supply regulate the price. In fact on an open market, speculation on the stock-exchange accrues. The open-market is separated into different submarkets by the criteria of the duration of the preliminary lead time. This time describes the latency between the initiation of a contract and its physical execution, in this case the delivery of electricity. The two submarkets are called futures- or exchange-market and spot-market. The market with the shorter preliminary lead time is the spot-market (cf. Ströbele et al. 2010, p. 230).

The submarket with the longer preliminary lead time, of usually more than one month up to seven years (cf. Borchert et al. 2006, p. 13), is the futures- or exchange-market. This submarket can be differentiated by the marketplace, on which the energy is dealt. On one hand the *on-market* trading, which consists of the classical stock-exchange trading. On the other hand the *beside-market* trading, this consists of the so called *Over-The-Counter* (OTC) trading (cf. Ströbele et al. 2010, p. 69).

To get a better idea about the different submarkets and their specifications, see figure 1, which illustrates the open-market model.

Figure 1: Open-Market Model Illustration

	Futuresmarket / Exchangemarket		Spotmarket	
Submarket	OTC	Stock-Exchange	Day-Ahead	Intraday
Marketplace	off-exchange	stock-exchange	stock-exchange	
Preliminary Lead-Time	several weeks up to several years		one day	less than one day

Source: own diagram, based on Ströbele et al. 2010, p. 230.

The largest amount of energy is traded on the so called OTC-markets. These markets are not linked to any stock exchanges. Bilateral contracts between users and suppliers are the most established method, how end customers get into contact with electricity markets. Usually these contracts have fixed prices per unit over the term of one or two years. Because of the long-term business relationship the daily or hourly changes in electricity prices are not relevant for the end customers, because they are not able to respond to them (cf. Lijesen, 2007, p. 254). Due to the long-time reference, these contracts are also called forward-contracts (cf. Borchert et al. 2006, p. 11).

The second possible marketplace of the futures-market is the stock-exchange market, where standardized contracts are traded. On the stock-exchange first of all bids by buyers and sellers are collected. Both transfer the information about the amount of energy they want to trade and for which price they would accept a deal. This happens hourly, so every day a new market price is computed for 24 times. The incoming bids are listed in ascending order, which results in a staircase-shaped demand-and supply-curve. A computer calculates the price, for which the largest possible amount of energy gets traded. A higher price would only be accepted by a few demanders and for a lower price only a few suppliers would be willing to deliver energy. This price is the so called clearing price, to which all deals are transacted. If a supplier bids a higher price than the clearing price, its offer will not be accepted, if he bids a lower price than the clearing price, he will receive the clearing price, which may be higher (cf. Borchert et al. 2006, p. 10 f.).

On the contrary to the futures-market with its long-term contracts, the spot market provides a platform for short-term electricity trading, also known as balancing-markets (cf. Conejo et al. 2010, p. 2). In Germany two kinds of spot-markets exist. The first one is the *Day-Ahead-Market* where deals with power deliveries for the following day are processed. This is one of the most important submarkets because usually the planning of the running of power plants is made one day before the actual production of electricity. The Day-Ahead-Market facilitates the trading of energy for particular hours. So buyers are able to cover their daily needs partly. The volume is with 0.1 MW much smaller than it is on the future market. The price is calculated hourly by the clearing house of the stock-exchange. As for the future-markets, they have the knowledge of the amount of all bids (cf. Ströbele et al. 2010, p. 231). The price finding on the day-ahead-market is similar to the stock-exchange market, it consists of three phases. First of all bids are submitted, afterwards the price is determined and based on that some bids get accepted and settled at the determined price (cf. Stoft, 2002, p. 218 f.).

The second submarket of the spot-market is the *Intraday-Market*, it has the shortest of all preliminary lead times. On the German Intraday-market e.g., electricity can be traded until 45 minutes before the physical fulfillment. The quantity traded on this market is much lower than on the others, because the energy packages traded on the Intraday-Market are small. Usually they are only used to cover individual short-term demand increases. This market is the last chance to trade energy before the markets close and the grid becomes under the control of the operator, monitoring the in- and output (cf. Ströbele et al. 2010, p. 231).

In course of time the variety and complexity of tradable products increased and more subjects participated in the market. Today e.g. the buyer is able to settle price barriers on the spot market. The so called *cap* implements the upper border, which restricts the maximum price, the buyer has to pay, even if the spot-price is higher. The buyer fixes a price maximum, he is inclined to pay, but he may still benefit of sinking prices. The opposite are the so called *floors*. They guarantee minimum revenue to the seller. To guarantee the functioning in the increasing complex markets, portfolio managers are installed to advise and administer the positions of smaller market participants, such as smaller municipal energy suppliers or industrial concerns. In total, the amount of these smaller participants is increasing because of the crowding-out-effect of the traditional monopole-structures (cf. Borchert et al. 2006, p. 16 f.).

3.2 The Pool-Market Model

The second big European electricity-trading model is the pool-market model. This model is distinguished by the existence of side payments of the open-market model. Energy generators give information about their marginal production costs and certain other variables like their production capacity into the pool. By doing this, they place a bid with the expectation to be accepted. In the pool a central pool manager is installed to solve the resulting allocation problem and to compute a price. Based upon this price some bids get accepted and the contract is created. If this price is lower than the marginal costs of some generators, they would incur a loss. To avoid this, the pool-market model makes side payments to cover these losses (cf. Stoft, 2002, p. 88 f.).

As the pool manager is responsible for calculating the market price, his task is the consideration of a sufficiently high enough side payment. Another task is to determine a surcharge to be able to compensate possible grid defiles (cf. Ströbele et al. 2010, p. 234 f.). Another instance in the pool model is the Transmission System Operator (TSO), whose responsibility is to guarantee the stability of the power grid to avoid blackouts or breakdowns. The TSO must be part of a non-commercial organization, to be free of economic interests (cf. NordPool Spot AS, 2013, p. 5).

The biggest European pool is NordPool, to whom the Scandinavian countries belong to (cf. Ströbele et al. 2010, p. 235 f.). NordPool is still expanding and affiliating new member states, like lastly Lithuania in June 2012 (cf. European Commission, 2012 A, p. 3). Today the six countries Denmark, Norway, Sweden, Finland, Estonia and Lithuania belong to NordPool. According to NordPool, they are running the leading power market in Europe and offer a day-ahead as well as an intraday trading platform where 370 companies out of 20 countries are trading (cf. NordPool Spot, 2013 A). Another central element of the pool-system is the constant exchange of electricity within the pool. To be more flexible Nord-

Pool separated the member-states into 14 different subareas, which can be seen in figure 2. The table on the upper left shows the production and the consumption of the individual areas.

Figure 2: NordPool Power System Overview

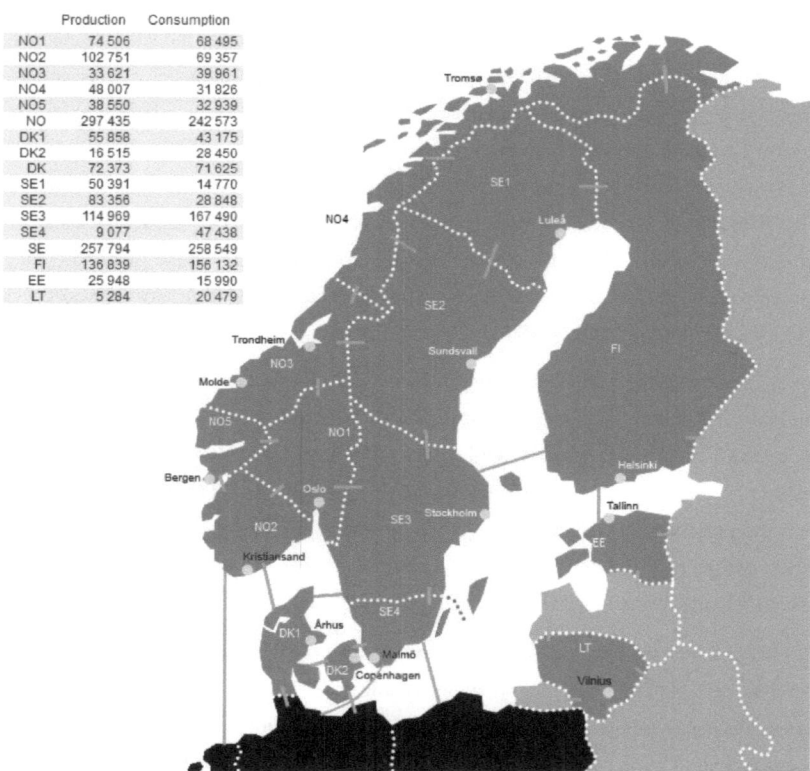

	Production	Consumption
NO1	74 506	68 495
NO2	102 751	69 357
NO3	33 621	39 961
NO4	48 007	31 826
NO5	38 550	32 939
NO	297 435	242 573
DK1	55 858	43 175
DK2	16 515	28 450
DK	72 373	71 625
SE1	50 391	14 770
SE2	83 356	28 848
SE3	114 969	167 490
SE4	9 077	47 438
SE	257 794	258 549
FI	136 839	156 132
EE	25 948	15 990
LT	5 284	20 479

As it can be seen, the NordPool-area is not a closed system; the grid infrastructure allows beside electricity-transmission between the areas also the transmission towards other areas, not belonging to NordPool. For additional real time information of the flows between all the market participants, the current market prices in the different subareas and the compounding of the generated energy mix see the following link, which is also findable on the homepage:

http://www.statnett.no/en/The-power-system/Production-and-consumption/State-of-the-Nordic-Power-System-Map/.

As mentioned above, NordPool offers a day-ahead spot-market, which is called *Elspot*. In practice Elspot is organised in a simple manner: Until noon of the day before the estimated delivery, the market participants are allowed to place bids about the amount of power they want to buy or sell. These bids are placed for every single hour at different price levels. On this basis the pool manager computes the corresponding market clearing prices. All accepted bids are settled at this clearing price (cf. Amundsen and Bergmann, 2003, p. 112 and NordPool Spot, 2013 B, p. 9 et seqq.).

The intraday-market in NordPool is called *Elbas*. On this market participants share information about the amount of electricity they want to sell and buy. Based on this, a contract is formed under a first-come, first-served basis. A specialty is the possible participation of other neighbour-countries like Germany or Benelux. If the intraday market has available transmission capacity after the pool-members placed their bids, the neighbour-countries are able to participate and to trade energy on this market, although they are not members of the NordPool region (cf. NordPool Spot AS, 2013 B, p. 14 et seqq. and Figure 2).

3.3   Discussion of the Two Models

The price calculation in both models is almost identical, prices result from quantities of supply and demand. One big difference between the open-market and the pool-model is that in the pool-model grid-bottlenecks are taken into account (cf. Ströbele et al. 2010, p. 235).

Discussion of the Open-Market-Model:

As it can be seen in figure 1, the stock-exchange covers the majority of the organization of the submarkets of the open-market. An advantage of energy-stock-exchanges is the exclusively acceptance of bids, which break even. Otherwise an agreement would not be signed. This results in highly efficient deals, made on these types of markets. But the stock-exchange orders are limited to fixed contracts; there is no flexibility to negotiate specific details about the deal. On the stock-exchange a bid about the commodity *energy* is placed. This commodity is very specific, the quality doesn't change, and it doesn't matter who appears as the supplier and who appears as the customer. This constellation results right in the moment when the deal takes place. So there is no need and no time to negotiate about contract details (cf. Borchert et al. 2006, p. 9 f. and Ströbele et al. 2010, p. 234 f.).

The OTC-markets, the second kind of the futures markets in the open-market-model, has no binding to specific contract details, like on the stock-exchange. The business partners are much more flexible in developing frame conditions of their contract. On the OTC-markets it is possible that energy is traded for the same point of time with different prices. No clearing price is calculated and the risk of nonfulfillment arises.

The risk of nonfulfillment is a disadvantage of both futures markets, because of the long preliminary lead times and unpredictable external influences, for example, environmental disasters or economical fluctuations may occur (cf. Ströbele et al. 2010, p. 69).

Discussion of the Pool-Model:

An advantage of the Pool-model is the consideration of grid-optimization by the pool manager. If at some places in the power grid, supply and demand drift apart and a non-optimal allocation would occur, the pool manager takes this into account and adapts the prices. Thus grid bottlenecks are considered in the price, which causes in an increase of the grid stability and finally the whole system can be optimized (cf. Ströbele et al. 2010, p. 235).

Another advantage of the Pool-model is the permanent computation of the clearing market price. On one hand this eliminates the risk that the buyer cannot pay for the ordered energy-delivery and on the other hand, the risk that the seller cannot deliver is eliminated as well. Both induce a calming of the markets (cf. Amundsen and Bergmann, 2003, p. 112).

But the pool-model has its disadvantages too. One is the possible acceptance of losing bids. This negative effect should be counterbalanced by the consideration of the in section 3.2 mentioned side-payment. Another disadvantage is the high complexity of the pool-model. Very exact optimization models are needed, to calculate efficient and economical market-prices. Because of the imperfection of the used mathematical model, the calculation will never deliver a perfectly efficient price. Hence the efficiency of the pool-model is highly dependent of the used mathematical model. Small errors in this model can cause huge price inefficiencies (cf. Stoft, 2002, p. 83 and Ströbele et al. 2010, p. 235).

As it has been shown, both models have their advantages and their disadvantages. The Pool-model offers incentives for energy-producers to build power plants in areas with higher energy prices, this helps to reduce bottlenecks in the grid-infrastructure (Ströbele et al. 2010, p. 235). So this model is suitable for large geographical areas, where electricity must be transported over long distances and there may be high requirements to keep the grid in a stable condition.

The open-market-model with its OTC and stock-exchange submarkets features highly efficient pricing structures on the stock-exchange on one hand and the possibility of individual delivery contracts on the other hand.

4   Development and Integration of Renewables on European Markets

The exhaustibility of fossil fuels forces mankind to find alternatives to satisfy the growing electricity-demand. In Europe the awareness for the necessity of a change in electricity markets has increased over the past decades. Green electricity became an important topic in national parliaments and ambitious targets for the development of renewable energies have been set up (cf. Gan et al. 2007, p. 153).

Discussions about power generation by renewable energies began in 1973 during the course of the oil crisis. Due to extremely high rising energy prices, caused by the reduction of oil supplies, the call for alternatives were getting louder. One year later the first programs for the development of wind turbine technology were launched. The main goal was to become independent of fossil energy resources (cf. Gan et al. 2007, p. 144).

International environmental treaties like the Kyoto protocol of 1997 reinforced the development from fossil energy resources towards natural resources. The usage of inexhaustible potentials like the sunlight led companies to completely new markets and industries. In 1991, policy took a step forward and the German government set up the first law to support the renewables development. This law guaranteed fixed tariffs for the long-term to minimize development risks for the firms, investing in these new industries (cf. Gan et al. 2007, p. 153). Compared to the rest of the European Union, the results were quite remarkable. Between 1991 and 2000 power generation from renewables grew by 142 % in Germany, compared to 25 % in the rest of the European Union. In the same period the share of renewables in Germany more than doubled from 2.8 to 6.3 % (cf. Wüstenhagen and Bilharz, 2006, p. 1689).

The key to success for the notable results in Germany was the early support of green power generation by the electorate and the politicians (cf. Gan et al. 2007, p. 153).

In the next years the trend towards renewables gained on intensity and simultaneously special challenges arose. Some renewables like wind generators or solar collectors entail a difficulty about the missing possibility to predict their output far in advance. This difficulty has an important impact on the market. Because the energy-output is unpredictable in the long run, short-term markets like day-ahead or the intraday market are of special relevance (cf. Klessmann et al. 2008, p. 3647).

Because of high R&D expenses and sunken costs because of fail developments the interest of investments in this sector is cautious. If the companies would sell the produced energy cost-covering, it would be too expensive to find customers on the markets. This dilemma needs to be solved by the support of governments. If they create favourable economic frame conditions for renewable industries, these high cost-intensive projects can become cost effective. Following the two different approaches of governmental support are described.

In Germany the producers of renewables sell the energy at a legally regulated price to the electricity suppliers. This system is called feed-in tariffs. In 2000 the German government adopted the *Erneuerbare Energien Gesetz* ("Renewable Energy Sources Act"), which guarantees long-term fixed feed-in tariffs and a priority feed-in. So the renewable producers can calculate with fixed revenue per KwH over a long time – for most of the renewables its 20 years – and the guarantee of a 100 % demand of their produced energy. Because of the fixed price for produced energy, the producers of renewables are not participating the electricity market in a financially manner. Accordingly changes in energy market prices are irrelevant for them. This establishes ideal frame conditions, supporting a steep growth in this sector in Germany, because the risk for renewable projects is minimized. But the German system has its disadvantages as well. The autonomy of the market prices result in a nontransparency because several DNOs (Distribution Network Operators) and four different TSOs (Transmission System Operators) are involved (better: intercalated?). Another weakness is the missing cost-optimization due to exorbitantly high prices, some TSOs call for (cf. Klessmann et al. 2008, p. 3650).

But nevertheless the fixed feed-in tariff system is effective. This is reflected in a continuous increase in the share of regenerative power. In 2011 20,35 % of the total gross-power-production in Germany were covered by the renewables, which is an increase of about 20,4 % relative to the previous year (cf. table 2 and BMU, 2012 A).

A different approach to support the development of the renewable industry is the feed-in premium. In this system the produced energy is sold on the electricity market via the power exchange or bilateral contracts. The suppliers of renewables get a feed-in premium on top of the market price. This premium is guaranteed by law. This system is used in Spain for example. Spanish producers of renewable energy have the choice between the fixed feed-in tariff system and the market price plus feed-in premium system. After a significant upswing in energy prices in Spain the Spanish government decided in 2007 to introduce boundaries to guarantee minimum revenue on the one hand and to limit the maximum value of market price plus premium on the other hand. The support for renewable projects by the government is existent, like in the German system. But in the beginning the Spanish system had an unrestricted risk of market price developments. After the law-revision in 2007 the risk became limited by the upper and lower boundaries. A big difference between the policies in Germany and Spain is the adaption of the amount of the tariff. In Germany the amount is flexible and depends on many factors, like used technology, geographical diversity (e.g.

15

hours of sunshine in different regions) and age of the plant. In Spain the amount is universal for each project and is recalculated every year. This bears the risk of in an over-/ or under-aid (cf. Klessmann et al. 2008, p. 3651 f. and BMU, 2005). Compared to the latest numbers of the German renewable development, the Spanish figures are even more impressive. In 2012 the share of gross-electricity-production was 30.18 %. In 2011 the share was 33.06 % (cf. table 2). The reason for the decrease may be the difficult economic situation in Spain. The higher level of renewable consumption in Spain may be caused by the perfect climatic conditions with many hours of sunshine and constant wind at the Spanish coasts.

Figure 3 shows the dependency of the governmental support for renewables (RES) as a function of the market price.

Figure 3: Role of the Market Price in different Schemes

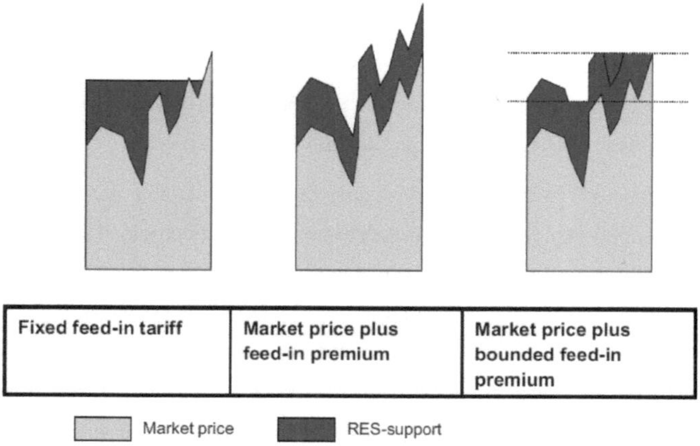

| Fixed feed-in tariff | Market price plus feed-in premium | Market price plus bounded feed-in premium |

□ Market price   ■ RES-support

Source: Klessmann et al. 2008, p. 3656.

5   Outlook and Conclusion

The main goals of the electricity market deregulation in Europe have been the reduction of governmental influences in this sector, the introduction of competition and an increase in the demand side participation by choosing between different energy providers. The liberalization of the electricity markets in all EU-member states, one of the main goals of the EU energy policy, has been achieved. The next big step is to merge the national electricity markets to a common European electricity market. This market must be based on competition, security of supply and the consideration of the environment (cf. Makkonen et al. 2012, p. 431).

To reach this goal a couple of difficulties need to be resolved. The European grid expansion is currently showing signs of very slow progress. Bottlenecks at the country borders are the consequence and this hampers market integration. The EU is aware of this problem and in its latest regulation (cf. Verordnung (EG) Nr. 714/2009) got captured that the *European Network of Transmission System Operators* (ENTSO) should elaborate a European-wide ten-year network development plan, on this basis regional and national grid reinforcement plans will be made (cf. Makkonen et al. 2012, p. 432).

The EU considers itself as a forerunner in the climate protection and the establishment of a multinational green policy. In 2007 the European leaders discussed energy-targets for the next few decades. In 2009 the so called *20-20-20*-objectives were enacted: A 20 % reduction in EU greenhouse gas emissions from 1990 levels, a 20 % share of EU energy consumption produced from renewables and a 20 % improvement of the EU's energy efficiency. All these objectives are set for 2020 (cf. European Commission, 2012 B).

It remains to be seen, if the *20-20-20*-objectives can be fulfilled, it is certain that adaptions on the electricity markets towards more competition and efficiency are necessary. Due to the nuclear disaster in Fukushima Daiichi after the tsunami in March 2011, the German government e.g. decided to change its energy mix radically. Three months after the catastrophe the government adopted an amendment in the Atomic Energy Law, which comprised the shutdown of the remaining nine nuclear power plants until 2022 (cf. BMU, 2012 B). On one hand this strengthens the necessity of the development of alternatives, but on the other hand, this results in a short-term increase of fossil fuels use.

In 2012 Makkonen et al. tried to estimate aspects, influencing the future of the electricity markets. They used the Delphi-Method as their experimental design, which is a qualitative research method to figure out future developments. In at least two question periods experts are asked to estimate the future influences of certain aspects. After every question period, they get these results as a basis for the next round. In this study a panel of experts served as the source of information. The panel consists of representatives of 15 European countries, whose job titles vary from advisor to vice-president (cf. Makkonen et al. 2012, p. 432).

The key objective of Makkonen et al. was to determine the prospects of European electricity markets until 2030. First the experts were asked anonymously to identify and categorize factors which are likely to influence the electricity market in the next few decades. This choice of the participants was made on their different expertise on electricity market knowledge (cf. Makkonen et al. 2012, p. 431 et seqq.).

As mentioned before, a large problem within the European grid is bottlenecks. The experts confirmed the removal of these bottlenecks as an important criterion for the development of a single European electricity market. In this point the experts see an increasing importance for the future market development. Investments in the transmission grid must be done very quickly; a delay in investments has already been the main reason for the existence of bottlenecks. According to the experts, these delays in investments, due to longsome permission procedures, must be reduced. The experts see the expansion of the transmission network mostly as a national problem. They even doubt that the competence of the *Agency for the Cooperation of Energy Regulators* (ACER) is enough to force network investments (cf. Makkonen et al. 2012, p. 435).

In the first question period the experts mentioned the transmission grid network problems as the most critical factor in the development of a single European Electricity Market. In the following round the experts suggested some approaches to resolve these difficulties. Beside a stronger role of the ACER, another possibility could be the simplification of the bureaucratic permitting procedures or the harmonization of regulatory processes (cf. Makkonen et al. 2012, p. 435 f.).

A second central point of the research of Makkonen et al. is the trade of electricity. At this point the experts agree that some progresses have been made in the past. The national differences between electricity trading systems are well-known and the development of common trading systems is quite advanced. Hence this isn't a critical aspect for the functioning of a single European Market (cf. Makkonen et al. 2012, p. 436).

Interesting is the case that on one hand a single European price area is not a central goal because the requirements for network investments would be too high. But on the other hand the experts agree that small price areas on the other hand contain problems for the competition as well (cf. Makkonen et al. 2012, p. 436 f.).

Another result of the Delphi study concerns the necessity of a supporting mechanism for the renewables. So the previously discussed problems from section 4 regarding expensive development and high R&D expenditures are still up-to-date and will remain up-to-date in the future. The experts are balanced with the question; if there will be common retail markets in Europe in 2030. They see the development of a technology which allows the storing of electricity economically and on a grand scale as the "wild card" which can relate to dramatically changes on the markets. This may reduce the volatility in electricity prices and would help to penetrate the development of the renewables (cf. Makkonen et al. 2012, p. 438).

But it should always be kept in mind, that the discovery of a new technology like an efficient possibility to accumulate energy in large-scales could revolutionize and change the market structure and the market development throughout Europe and furthermore dramatically.

So in my opinion the main approach to develop a single European electricity market and to be steeled for the future is to focus on the support of new technologies (especially renewables), the reduction of market restraints and the development of homogenous and explicit market frame conditions.

Bibliography

Amundsen, E. S.; Bergmann, L. (2003): The deregulated electricity markets in Norway and Sweden: a tentative assessment. In: Competition in European Electricity Markets – A Cross-country Comparison (ed.), by Glachant, J. M. and Finon, D. F., 110-132.

Arus, I. (2013): Electricity Market – A place for Electricity Producers and Consumers, http://elering.ee/electricity-market-opening/ (created: unknown, downloaded: 05/20/2013).

BMU (Bundesministerium für Umwelt, Naturschutz und Reaktorsicherheit), (2012, A): Erneuerbare Energien auch im Jahr 2012 weiter angewachsen, http://www.erneuerbare-energien.de/die-themen/datenservice/erneuerbare-energien-in-zahlen/erneuerbare-energien-im-jahr-2012/ (created: unknown, downloaded: 05/15/2013).

BMU (Bundesministerium für Umwelt, Naturschutz und Reaktorsicherheit), (2012, B): Die Entwicklungen in Deutschland nach der Reaktorkatastrophe in Japan, http://www.bmu.de/themen/atomenergie-strahlenschutz/atomenergie-sicherheit/fukushima-folgemassnahmen/ueberblick/ (created: 03/2012, downloaded: 05/12/2013).

BMU (Bundesministerium für Umwelt, Naturschutz und Reaktorsicherheit), (2005): Ein-speisesysteme in Spanien und Deutschland und ein Vergleich, http://www.erneuerbare-energien.de/unser-service/mediathek/downloads/detailansicht/artikel/einspeisesysteme-in-spanien-und-deutschland-und-ein-ver-gleich/?tx_ttnews[backPid]=608&cHash=bd71c0c9c0c455893c9770891ac958f1&sword_list[]=Einspeisesysteme&sword_list[]=in&sword_list[]=Spanien&no_cache=1 (created: 06/2005, downloaded: 05/15/2013).

Borchert, J.; Schemm, R.; Korth, S. (2006): Stromhandel. Institutionen, Marktmodelle, Pricing and Risikomanagement, Schäffer-Poeschel Verlag, Stuttgart, Germany.

20

Chick, M. (2007): Electricity and Energy Policy in Britain, France and the United States since 1951, Edward Elgar, Cheltenham, UK.

Conejo, A. J.; Carrión, M.; Morales, Juan M. (2010): Decision Making Under Uncertainty in Electricity Markets. In: International Series in Operations Research & Management Science, 153, 1-26.

European Commission (2012 A): Quarterly Report on European Electricity Markets, Vol. 1-4 of 2012. http://ec.europa.eu/energy/observatory/electricity/electricity_en.htm (created: unknown, downloaded: 05/10/2013).

European Commission (2012 B): The EU climate and energy package, http://ec.europa.eu/clima/policies/package/index_en.htm (created: 09/10/2012, downloaded: 05/18/2013).

Gan, L.; Eskeland, G. S.; Kolshus, H. H. (2007): Green electricity market development: Lessons from Europe and the US. In: Energy Policy, 35(1), 144-155.

Joskow, Paul L. (2008): Lessons learned from electricity market liberalization. In: The Energy Journal, 29(2), 9-42.

Klessmann, C.; Nabe, C.; Burges, K. (2008): Pros and cons of exposing renewables to electricity market risks – A comparison of the market integration approaches in Germany, Spain and the UK. In: Energy Policy, 36(10), 3646-3661.

Lijesen, M. G. (2007): The real-time price elasticity of electricity. In: Energy Economics, 29, 249-258.

Makkonen, M.; Pätäri, S.; Jantunen, A.; Viljainen, S. (2012): Competition in the European electricity markets – outcomes of a Delphi study. In: Energy Policy, 44, 431-444.

Meeus, L.; Purchala, K.; Belmans, R. (2005): Development of the Internal Electricity Market in Europe. In: The Electricity Journal, 18(6), 25-35.

NordPool Spot (2013 A): http://www.nordpoolspot.com/About-us/ (created: unknown, downloaded: 05/14/2013).

NordPool Spot (2013 B):
http://www.nordpoolspot.com/Global/Download%20Center/Rules-and-regulations/The-Nordic-Electricity-Exchange-and-the-Nordic-model-for-a-liberalized-electricity-market.pdf (created: unknown, downloaded: 05/14/2013).

NordPool Spot AS (2013): The Nordic Electricity Exchange and The Nordic Model for a Liberalized Electricity Market,
http://www.nordpoolspot.com/Global/Download%20Center/Rules-and-regulations/The-Nordic-Electricity-Exchange-and-the-Nordic-model-for-a-liberalized-electricity-market.pdf, (created: unknown, downloaded: 05/20/2013).

Stoft, S. (2002): Power System Economics. Designing Markets for Electricity, 1. Edition, John Wiley & Sons, Piscataway.

Ströbele, W.; Pfaffenberger, W.; Heuterkes, M. (2010): Energiewirtschaft: Einführung in Theorie und Politik, 2. Auflage, Oldenbourg Verlag München.

Verordnung (EG) Nr. 714/2009 des europäischen Parlaments und des Rates. In: Amtsblatt der Europäischen Union, L 211/16 (9).

von Koppenfels (2010): Mehr Wettbewerb durch wirksame Entflechtung der Strom- und Gasversorgungsnetze – Das dritte Liberalisierungspaket zum Energiebinnenmarkt der Europäischen Union. In: Dratwa, F. A.; Ebers, M.; Pohl, A. K.; Spiegel, B.; Strauch, G. (ed.), Energiewirtschaft in Europa – Im Spannungsfeld zwischen Klimapolitik, Wettbewerb und Versorgungssicherheit. Springer-Verlag Berlin Heidelberg. pp.77-89.

Wüstenhagen, R.; Bilharz, M. (2006): Green energy market development in Germany: effective public policy and emerging customer demand. In: Energy Policy, 34(13), 1681-1696.

Zenke, I.; Schäfer R. (2012): Einleitung: Der Großhandel von Energie und Energieträgern in Europa. In: Zenke, I.; Schäfer R. (ed.): Energiehandel in Europa: Öl, Gas, Strom, Derivate, Zertifikate. Verlag C. H. Beck, München, pp. 1-10.

Table 2: Electricity-Generation by Renewables in % - Annually Data

Letzte Aktualisierung   11.02.13
Exportierte Daten   28.05.13
Quelle der Daten   Eurostat
UNIT   Percent

GEO/TIME	2006	2007	2008	2009	2010	2011
Europäische Union (27 Länder)	14,24	15,14	16,36	18,25	19,94	20,44
Europäische Union (25 Länder)	13,97	15,02	16,25	18,18	19,74	20,54
Belgien	3,08	3,65	4,62	6,08	6,79	9,04
Bulgarien	11,18	7,52	7,42	9,81	15,15	9,8
Tschechische Republik	4,91	4,73	5,18	6,78	8,32	10,3
Dänemark	23,97	27,04	26,7	27,49	33,11	38,81
Deutschland (bis 1990 früheres Gebiet der BRD)	11,37	14,11	14,63	16,2	16,9	20,35
Estland	1,45	1,48	2,04	6,11	10,75	12,64
Irland	8,46	9,46	11,69	14,13	12,83	19,4
Griechenland	11,82	6,77	8,29	12,45	16,68	12,99
Spanien	17,58	19,45	20,58	25,83	33,06	30,18
Frankreich	12,17	12,96	14,07	13,62	14,45	12,84
Italien	14,1	13,25	16,19	20,54	22,23	23,64
Zypern	0,02	0,06	0,27	0,07	0,7	2,53
Lettland	37,65	36,39	41,21	49,23	48,47	41,93
Litauen	3,61	4,6	4,65	5,5	7,76	9,63
Luxemburg	3,12	3,33	3,58	3,66	3,09	2,95
Ungarn	3,47	4,29	5,36	6,99	7,09	6,35
Malta	0,0	0,0	0,0	0,0	0,0	0,0
Niederlande	6,71	6,18	7,72	9,15	9,26	10,09
Österreich	57,45	60,72	62,3	67,69	61,41	55,23
Polen	2,85	3,53	4,27	5,8	6,97	8,3
Portugal	28,86	29,63	26,42	33,27	49,99	43,62
Rumänien	31,43	26,86	28,37	27,91	34,18	27,05
Slowenien	24,43	22,13	29,11	36,76	33,13	26,2
Slowakei	16,51	16,57	15,48	17,88	20,51	17,01
Finnland	23,96	25,92	30,78	25,77	26,52	27,65
Schweden	47,55	51,54	54,98	56,44	54,48	58,72
Vereinigtes Königreich	4,47	4,88	5,4	6,63	6,71	9,2
Island	99,96	:	:	:	:	:
Norwegen	98,33	106,12	109,42	103,01	89,96	97,92
Schweiz	48,14	55,38	55,05	55,85	54,81	:
Kroatien	33,4	23,0	27,92	36,89	45,05	25,62
Die ehemalige jugoslawische Republik Mazedonien	18,74	11,24	9,29	15,36	27,99	:
Türkei	25,49	19,19	17,38	19,65	26,47	25,22

Source: Eurostat, http://epp.eurostat.ec.europa.eu/portal/page/portal/eurostat/home/, downloaded: 28.05.2013

24